DESIGNING
Digital
Games

by Derek Breen

WILEY

DESIGNING DIGITAL GAMES

Published by
John Wiley & Sons, Inc.
111 River Street
Hoboken, NJ 07030-5774
www.wiley.com

CONTENTS

PROJECT 3: A-MAZE-ING GAME 51

PROJECT 4: ATTACKING THE CLONES 79

AUTHOR NOTES 114

INTRODUCTION ALL ABOUT SCRATCH

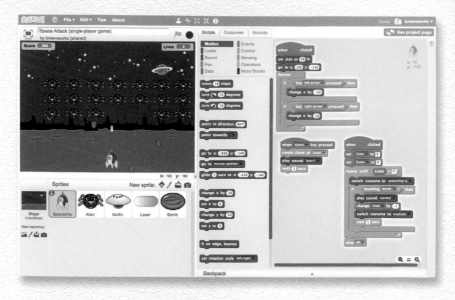

While many tools out there allow you to create digital games, this book focuses on Scratch because Scratch is the very best! Just kidding . . . who can say which is the best? Of course, that is just MY opinion. But Scratch is certainly ONE of the best applications for rapidly designing your own videogames, whether you are an 11-year-old boy, an 8-year-old girl or a 45-year-old bald guy.

There is no one right way to start using Scratch, so you can begin with any project in this book. But if you have never used Scratch before, I suggest starting with Project 1 (which is far less lame than you might think).

Before making your first game, I suggest browsing the online Scratch community (scratch.mit.edu) to see the wide variety of game projects people have made using Scratch. Please share your own game when you are finished and be sure to give credit to Derek Breen for the way his AMAZING BOOK made you the proud game designer you are! (Or not.)

Scratch was created for YOU and the designers at the MIT Media Lab had several goals:

1 **Give you powerful software for free.**

2 **Make it easy for you to learn.**

3 **Allow many different ways for you to use the software.**

4 **Enable you to browse/play/remix other projects.**

5 **Enable you to share your projects.**

6 **Create an online community where you can learn from one another.**

ABOUT THIS BOOK

Can I tell you a secret? You know what is more valuable than money? Time! I am being completely honest. You can spend your time *all kinds* of ways, and once you "spend" it, just like when you spend ten dollars, you never get it back. Guess what? That goes for me, too. If I am going to spend several months writing about Scratch, then I want to make sure I am producing a book that is genuinely going to help you learn some REALLY cool stuff!

Now let me make a deal with you; if you are willing to invest your time by reading even one project in this book, I will do my very best to get you making an addictive video game ASAP. You will hardly even need to *read*. Seriously, you can follow along as little or as much as you want and still end up with a KILLER project!

ICONS USED IN THIS BOOK

 The Tip icon marks tips and shortcuts that you can use to make coding easier.

The Warning icon tells you to watch out! It marks important information that may save you from scratching your head a ton.

The Remember icon marks concepts you've encountered before and should keep in mind while coding.

The Fun with Math icon describes the everyday math you use while coding computer programs. Finally, you see how that stuff really is used!

The Fun with Code icon describes how the coding you're doing relates to the bigger picture of computer programming.

ACCESS SCRATCH ON YOUR COMPUTER

The easiest way to start using Scratch is to visit scratch.mit.edu, create an online account, and start Scratching. To use Scratch without creating an account, you will have to download and install the offline version of Scratch (see the upcoming "Use Scratch Offline" section).

Technically, you can use the Scratch website without an account, but you will have to save projects to your computer and then upload them each time you visit the Scratch website to continue working on them. With an account, you can save files online and share projects with other Scratch users.

CREATE ONLINE ACCOUNT

Go ahead and start up Scratch! Turn on your computer, open a web browser, and visit scratch.mit.edu. If you already have a

Scratch account, click the Sign In button in the top-right corner of the page. If you do not have an account, click the Join Scratch button and fill in the brief online form. If you are under 13 or do not have an email account, please ask an adult to help you create an account (or skip ahead to the upcoming "Use Scratch Offline" section).

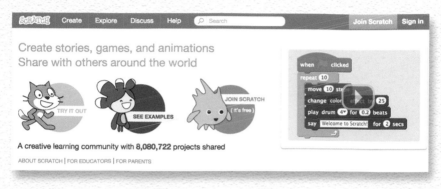

 To run Scratch online, you need a relatively recent web browser (Chrome 35 or later, Firefox 31 or later, or Internet Explorer 8 or later) with Adobe Flash Player version 10.2 or later installed. Scratch 2 is designed to support screen sizes 1024 x 768 or larger.

USE SCRATCH OFFLINE

You can install the Scratch 2 Offline Editor to work on projects without requiring a Scratch user account. After Scratch 2 is installed, you will not need an Internet connection to work on projects. This version will work on Mac, Windows, and some versions of Linux (32 bit). Visit scratch.mit.edu/scratch2download to download and install Adobe Air (required to run Scratch offline) and the Scratch 2 Offline Editor.

SCRATCH   Create   Explore   Discuss   Help   🔍 Search   Join Scratch   Sign in

Scratch 2 Offline Editor

You can install the Scratch 2.0 editor to work on projects without an internet
connection. This version will work on Mac, Windows, and some versions of
Linux (32 bit).

Adobe AIR	Scratch Offline Editor	Support Materials
If you don't already have it, download and install the latest Adobe AIR	Next download and install the Scratch 2.0 Offline Editor	Need some help getting started? Here are some helpful resources.
Mac OS X - Download ⬇	Mac OS X - Download ⬇	Starter Projects - Download ⬇
Mac OS 10.5 & Older - Download ⬇	Mac OS 10.5 & Older - Download ⬇	Getting Started Guide - Download 🗋
Windows - Download ⬇	Windows - Download ⬇	Scratch Cards - Download 🗋
Linux - Download ⬇	Linux - Download ⬇	

PROJECT 1 DESIGN A CLASSIC VIDEOGAME

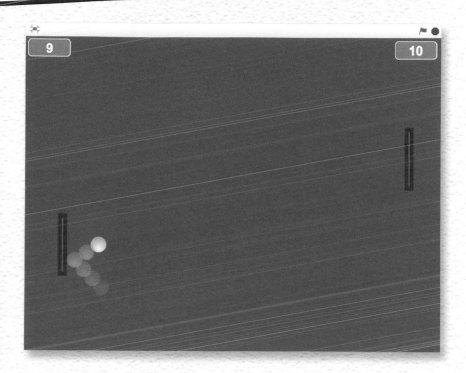

CREATING A CLASSIC PONG-STYLE VIDEOGAME IS THE GAME DESIGN EQUIVALENT TO STICK-FIGURE ANIMATION.

It's not so much about creating an awesome game as it is about covering the basic game design elements that you will need to create *your* awesome game. Most ball sports videogames (think tennis and soccer) evolved from *Pong,* so this is the perfect project for those of you who eventually want to design your own football, volleyball, basketball, or hockey game.

CREATE A NEW PROJECT

Because the name *Pong* is short for Ping-Pong and a bunch of people have been sued (by the inventors of *Pong*) for calling their games Pong, why not call your game *Ping-Pong*. (See how super-creative I am?)

1 Go to scratch.mit.edu and open the Scratch 2 Offline Editor.

2 If you are online, click Create. If you're offline, choose File ⇨ New.

3 Name your project. (If online, select the title and type Ping-Pong. If offline, chose File ⇨ Save As and type Ping-Pong.)

4 Delete that cat by selecting the Scissors and clicking the cat or by Shift-clicking the cat and choosing Delete.

With the cat gone, you have a world of possibilities!

CHANGE THE BACKGROUND COLOR

Paint your backdrop dark green, just like a classic ping-pong table.

1 Click the Backdrops tab. (You may need to click the Stage icon if you have any sprites selected in your project.)

2 Click the Fill with Color tool.

3 Click the Fill option to the left of the color swatches.

4 Click the color swatch you wish to use.

5 Click inside the Paint Editor canvas to fill the backdrop with the new color.

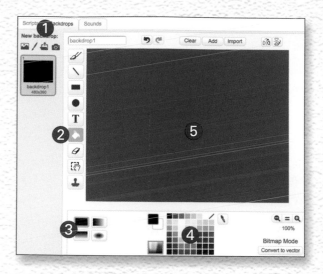

ADD A BOUNCING BALL

Even though it is not difficult to draw a ball, using the sprite named *Ball* in the Sprite Library will ensure everybody starts with the same sized sprite.

1 In the New Sprite area beneath the Stage, click the first icon: Choose Sprite from Library.

2 Under Category, click Things.

3 Click the sprite named Ball and then click the OK button.

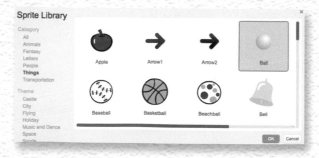

CHANGE THE BALL COLOR

On the Costumes tab delete all but the original orange costume, which looks more like a real ping-pong ball.

1 Click the costume you wish to delete.

2 Click the X that appears on the top-left corner of the costume.

3 Repeat for the other costumes you're deleting.

MAKE THE BALL MOVE

One block can move a sprite across the screen.

1 Click the Scripts tab.

2 Click the *Motions* category.

3 Click the MOVE 10 STEPS block, drag it into the Scripts Area, and then release the mouse or trackpad button.

4 Click the block one time while watching the ball on the Stage.

Each time you click the block, the ball should move ten steps to the right.

To start the game when the Green Flag is clicked:

1 On the Scripts tab, click the *Events* category.

2 Click and drag the WHEN GREEN FLAG CLICKED block into the Scripts Area.

3 Snap the block onto the top of the MOVE block.

When you click the Green Flag button, the ball should move ten steps.

MAKE BLOCKS REPEAT

Several blocks can make something happen over and over. Which one should you try?

1 In the *Control* category, find the FOREVER block.

2 Click and drag the FOREVER block over to snap beneath the WHEN GREEN FLAG CLICKED block.

Notice how the FOREVER block stretches to surround the MOVE block.

3 Click the Green Flag button to test your code.

Any blocks inside the FOREVER block will keep running as long as the Green Flag is on. But your ball will move only until it reaches the right side of the Stage. You haven't given the ball the instruction to bounce!

BOUNCE OFF EDGES

You just need one more block to make the ball bounce between edges of the Stage.

1 Click and drag the IF ON EDGE, BOUNCE block from the *Motion* category to the Scripts Area.

2 Snap it into place inside the FOREVER block, just beneath the MOVE block.

3 Click the Green Flag button to test your code.

Placing the IF ON EDGE, BOUNCE block inside the FOREVER block should make your ball bounce back and forth. But it's kinda boring to keep bouncing in a straight line.

CHANGE THE BOUNCE ANGLE

By default, all sprites are pointing in the same direction, to the right, but you are not stuck with this direction.

1 Click and drag the POINT IN DIRECTION block into the Scripts Area.

2 Snap the POINT IN DIRECTION block between WHEN GREEN FLAG CLICKED and FOREVER.

3 Click 90 to select it and type 45.

If you click the Green Flag button to test your code, the ball should now start traveling diagonally and then bounce in a different direction each time it reaches the edge of the Stage.

SET THE BALL STARTING POSITION AND SIZE

The ball should begin in the center of the screen and look a bit too large.

1 On the Scripts tab, click the *Motion* category, drag a GO TO X Y block into the Scripts Area, and then snap the GO TO X Y block to the bottom of the WHEN GREEN FLAG CLICKED block.

2 Change each number value to 0 (so the ball will start at X: 0, Y: 0).

3 Click the *Looks* category and drag a SET SIZE TO block into the Scripts Area.

4 Snap the SET SIZE TO block between WHEN GREEN FLAG CLICKED and GO TO blocks.

5 Change the SET SIZE TO value to 40 to decrease the ball's size from 100% to 40%.

6 Click the Green Flag button to test your code.

The ball should be smaller and begin at the center of the screen when the Green Flag button is pressed.

ADD THE PADDLES

If you are getting used to sprites and code blocks, you can pick up the pace a little when adding the game's paddles.

 1 Beneath the Stage, click the Choose Sprite from Library icon.

2 Chose the *Things* category.

3 Click the sprite named Paddle and then click the OK button.

 4 Click the Costumes tab, click the Color a Shape tool, choose a color swatch (I'll choose brown), and click inside the paddle.

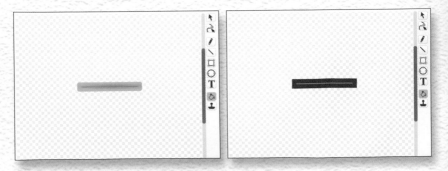

The paddle is the right shape and size, but needs to be rotated.

 1 On the Costumes tab, click the Select tool.

2 On the Paint Editor canvas, click the paddle.

3 Click the small circle that appears directly above the paddle and rotate the paddle into a vertical position.

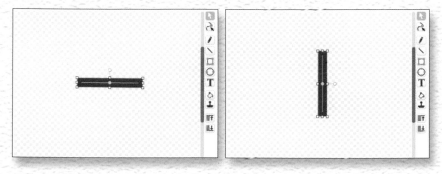

MOVE PADDLE WITH THE KEYBOARD

To play the game, players will use one key to move their paddle up and another key to move their paddle down. Before adding the code to enable this, you should position one paddle along one side of the screen.

1 On the Scripts tab, drag the WHEN GREEN FLAG CLICKED block into the Scripts Area.

2 From the *Motion* category, drag and snap a GO TO X Y block to the bottom of the WHEN GREEN FLAG CLICKED block.

3 Change the block values to X: 200 and Y: 0.

4 Click the Green Flag button to test your code.

Your paddle should move to the middle of the right side of the screen, leaving a gap between the paddle and the edge of the screen so there is room for the ball to zoom by. Now comes the really cool part: interactivity!

1 **Drag these blocks into the paddle's Scripts Area:**

2 **Inside the WHEN KEY PRESSED block, click the dropdown menu and choose *Up Arrow*.**

3 **Change the CHANGE Y BY block's value to 10.**

Instead of dragging more code blocks over for the Down-Arrow key, try this:

1 **Shift-click the WHEN UP ARROW KEY PRESSED block inside the Scripts Area and select Duplicate.**

2 **Drag the duplicate away from the original and then release the mouse or trackpad to drop the set of blocks.**

3 **Change Up Arrow to Down Arrow in the new WHEN KEY PRESSED block and change 10 to −10 in the new CHANGE Y BY block.**

Test your Up- and Down-Arrow keys to make sure your paddle moves up and down.

MAKE THE BALL BOUNCE OFF THE PADDLE

When you click the Green Flag button, the ball bounces off the edges but passes right through the paddle. Similar to the way you instruct the ball to bounce off the edge of the Stage, you must also instruct the ball to bounce off other objects.

1 Click the Ball sprite and then click the Scripts tab.

2 Drag an IF THEN block from the *Control* category and a TOUCHING? block from the *Sensing* category into the Scripts Area.

3 Insert the TOUCHING? block into the IF THEN block.

4 Click the drop-down menu inside the TOUCHING? block and choose Paddle.

5 Drag and snap a TURN CLOCKWISE block from the *Motion* category into the Scripts Area and inside the IF THEN block.

6 Change the TURN value to 180 (so the ball will move in the opposite direction).

7 Click and drag the IF THEN block inside the FOREVER block, just beneath the IF ON EDGE BOUNCE block.

When you click the Green Flag to test your game, the ball should bounce right off the paddle.

ADD A SECOND PLAYER

The game will surely be more fun with an opponent. Remember how to Shift-click a chunk of code to duplicate it? You can use the same technique to duplicate sprites, too. And, when you duplicate a sprite, all the code inside it is also duplicated. So it should be easy to create a second player.

1 **Shift-click the paddle sprite, choose *Info,* and change the name to *Player Right* (since it is on the right side of the Stage).**

◀2 **Click the blue triangle to exit *Info.***

3 **Shift-click *Player Right* and choose *Duplicate.***

4 **Shift click the new sprite, choose *Info,* and change the name to *Player Left.***

◀5 **Click the blue triangle to exit *Info.***

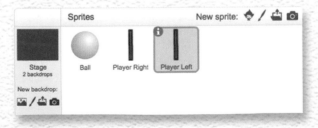

Go to the Scripts tab for *Player Left.* All the scripts from *Player Right* should be there.

UPDATE THE PLAYER LEFT CODE BLOCKS

1 Change the GO TO X Y block's X value to **-200**.

2 Change WHEN UP ARROW KEY PRESSED to WHEN W KEY PRESSED.

3 Change WHEN DOWN ARROW KEY PRESSED to WHEN S KEY PRESSED.

4 Click the Green Flag button to test your game.

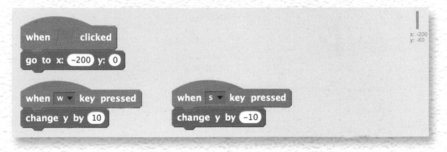

You probably noticed there's a problem: The ball bounces off *Player Right* but passes right through *Player Left*.

UPDATE THE BALL CODE

Scratch updated the TOUCHING? block when you changed the name of the sprite from *Paddle* to *Player Right*. But the IF THEN block is only checking whether the ball is touching *Player Right*, not *Player Left*.

1 Shift-click the IF THEN block, choose *Duplicate,* and drag the copy to snap beneath the original IF THEN block.

2 In the duplicate blocks, change *Player Right* to *Player Left*.

3 Click the Green Flag to test your code.

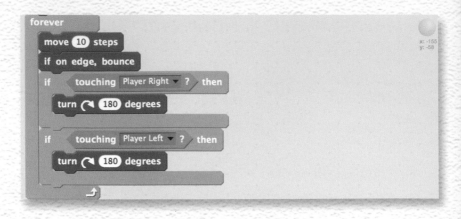

The ball should bounce off both rackets.

MAKE THE BOUNCE MORE RANDOM

You can use the PICK RANDOM block to choose a number between two different values.

1 Click the *Ball* sprite.

2 Click the Scripts tab.

3 Drag a PICK RANDOM block inside each TURN CLOCKWISE block (replacing the *180* values inside each) and change the values to match the following image:

Now when you click the Green Flag button to test your code, the ball should bounce off each racket at a slightly different angle.

KEEP TRACK OF PLAYER SCORES

So far, you have *Player Right* controlling one paddle and *Player Left* controlling a second paddle, with the ball just bouncing all over the place. If I am *Player Right* and you are *Player Left*, how do you score against me?

1 Click the *Ball* sprite and then click the Scripts tab.

2 Drag these three blocks into the Scripts Area:

Player1's X position is 200 and the maximum value is 240, so your IF THEN block could check whether the ball's X position is greater than 230 (it's good to have a little leeway). Type **230** inside the second > slot (IF X > 230).

CREATE SCORE VARIABLES

Variables provide a place for Scratch to keep track of the score for each player.

1 With the *Ball* sprite selected, click the *Data* category on the Scripts tab.

2 Click the Make a Variable button.

3 Name the variable *Player Right Score*, leave *For All Sprites* checked, and click OK.

4 Repeat Steps 2 and 3 to create a second variable named *Player Left Score.*

Both variables should appear on the Stage and you should now see several VARIABLE blocks listed under the *Data* category.

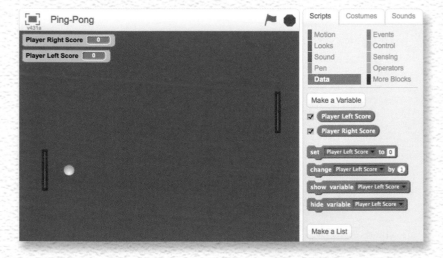

Double-click variables on the Stage to change how they display and click-and-drag to change where they display.

INCREASE THE SCORE

If *Player Left* misses the ball, then *Player Right*'s score should change by 1.

1 Drag and snap the CHANGE BY block from the *Data* category into the IF THEN block and change the values to *Player Left Score* and *1.*

2 Drag the IF THEN block into the FOREVER block so Scratch will continually check whether the ball has made it past *Player Right.*

3 Click the Green Flag button to test your code.

```
turn ↺ 180 degrees

if    x position > 230  then
    change Player Left Score ▾ by 1

    ↵
```

You must reset the position of the ball after adding a point or the score will keep increasing:

1 Drag and snap a GO TO X Y block to the bottom of the CHANGE BY block and set the values to X: 0 and Y: 0.

2 Drag and snap a WAIT SECS block from the *Control* category to the bottom of the GO TO X Y block and change the value to 1.

3 Click the Green Flag button to test your game.

```
turn ↺ 180 degrees

if    x position > 230  then
    change Player Left Score ▾ by 1
    go to x: 0 y: 0
    wait 1 secs

    ↵
```

Player 2's score should increase by 1 whenever the ball reaches the right side. Then the ball should jump to the center and wait 1 second before moving again.

Follow the same steps to enable Player 1's score whenever Player 2 misses the ball. Or you can take a shortcut by duplicating the previous code and changing the values. (Be sure to replace the > block with a < block!)

```
if      x position  < -230    then
    change Player Right Score ▼ by 1
    go to x: 0 y: 0
    wait 1 secs
```

RESET SCORES WHEN THE GAME STARTS

You will want to reset the score whenever somebody clicks the Green Flag button to start a new game. This is an *easy* one!

1 Click the *Ball* sprite and then click the Scripts tab.

2 Drag and snap these blocks into the Scripts Area beneath a WHEN GREEN FLAG CLICKED block and change the values to *Player Right Score* and *Player Left Score:*

```
when      clicked
set  Player Right Score ▼ to 0
set  Player Left Score ▼ to 0
set size to 40 %
```

CHECK FOR THE WINNING SCORE

Create a new sprite named *Game Over,* which will check the score, display a "Game Over" message when either player score reaches 11, and then end the game.

1 Click the Paint New Sprite icon beneath the Stage.

2 Click the Costumes tab.

Convert to vector **3** Click the Convert to Vector button.

T **4** Click the Text tool.

5 Select a font. (I'll select Helvetica.)

6 Choose a bright color swatch. (I'll choose orange to match the score color.)

7 Click near the center of the Paint Editor canvas and type Game Over!

On the Stage, you will need to click and drag the message into the correct position (centered and a bit above the ball).

ADD AN END-OF-GAME CODE

When one of the player's score reaches 11, the winning message should appear.

1 Click the Scripts tab for the *Game Over* sprite.

2 Add these blocks to the Scripts Area:

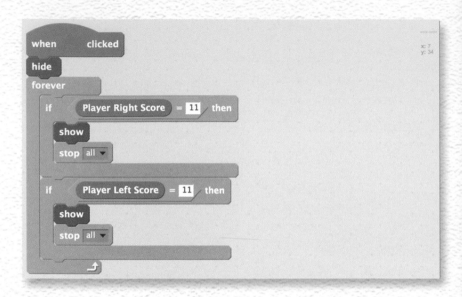

When you click the Green Flag button to test your code, you should be able to play the game until one of the players reaches 11, then the Game Over message should be displayed and the code should stop running. (Reduce the winning score if you want to check your code quickly without having to reach 11.)

You can improve your game by adding sound effects, including obstacles and adding new features like being able to catch the ball.

IMPROVE YOUR GAME

In game design, there is almost always room for improvement. In each of the next project, you will learn more game design techniques. In the meantime, see if you can figure out how to improve your Ping-Pong game. Here are a few ideas:

» **Make the goals smaller:** Instead of using the entire side you could create a smaller goal, as in ice hockey, to make it more difficult to score a point.

» **Add obstacles:** Add other sprites for the ball to bounce off between the two players.

» **Adjust game difficulty:** You can make the game more challenging by changing the length of the paddles, increasing the speed of the ball, or slowing down player movement.

» **Allow players to "catch" the ball:** Program an additional key players can press when the ball is close enough to catch. When they release the key, the ball could fly right across the Stage.

PROJECT 2 SUPER SNAKE

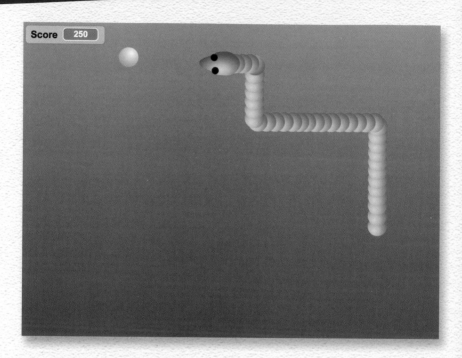

WAY BACK WHEN THERE WERE ONLY A FEW GAMES AVAILABLE FOR CELLPHONES, BEFORE THERE WERE EVEN SMARTPHONES, YOU COULD STILL PLAY THIS KIND OF ADDICTIVE/FUN/ INFURIATING GAME. And, you can create the entire project with just two sprites and a dash of Scratch blocks!

CREATE A NEW PROJECT

1 Go to scratch.mit.edu or open the Scratch 2 Offline Editor.

2 If you are online, click Create. If offline, select File ⇨ New.

3 Name your project. (If online, select the title and type Super Snake. **If using the offline version of Scratch, select File ⇨ Save As and type** Super Snake.)

4 Delete the cat by selecting the Scissors and clicking the sprite or holding the Shift key while clicking and then choosing *Delete.*

USE GRADIENT FOR BACKGROUND

You can make your backdrop a bit more interesting by using a gradient to blend between a lighter and a darker shade.

1 Click the Backdrops tab.

2 Click the Fill with Color tool.

3 Click one of the gradient options to the left of the color swatches.

4 Click a dark color swatch.

5 Click the current swatch to switch to the background color.

6 Choose a lighter color.

7 Click the Paint Editor canvas to fill the backdrop with your gradient.

8 If you wish to try a different gradient, click the Clear button and start over.

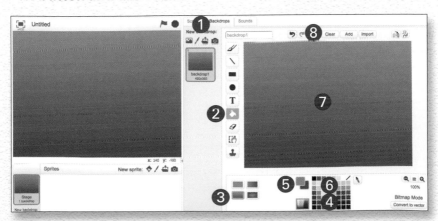

CONSTRUCT YOUR SNAKE

If you browse the Sprite Library, you will find many animals, but no snakes. That's fine. Part of the fun of this project is designing a slithering snake out of a few simple shapes.

1 **Click the Choose Sprite from Library icon beneath the Stage.**

2 **Choose the *Things* category.**

3 **Click the sprite named *Ball* and then click the OK button.**

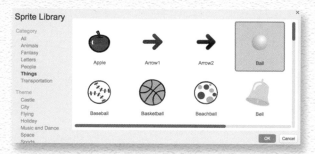

Wait until you see how Scratch lets you transform a simple ball into a sly serpent.

1 **Rename the sprite *Snake.* (Click the blue Info button or Shift-click and choose *Info.*)**

2 **Check which direction the sprite is facing (90 degrees to the right) so you know which side of the shape is the front of the head.**

3 **Click the Back button (white triangle on blue circle) to close the Info window.**

SELECT A SPRITE COSTUME

On the Costumes tab, click the color you wish to use for your snake and delete the other costumes. It will help later if you rename the costume to *Head*.

CREATE A SNAKE BODY

Instead of drawing the entire snake, you will use a few Scratch blocks to clone a simple body segment into a longer snake. Begin by duplicating the head costume.

1 **On the Costumes tab, Shift-click or right-click the first costume and choose *Duplicate*.**

2 **Rename the new costume *Body*.**

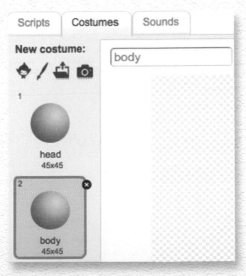

SCULPT THE SNAKE'S HEAD

The sprite you chose is a vector graphic, so you can use the Reshape tool to stretch it into a more familiar head shape.

1 Click the *Head* costume.

2 Click the Reshape tool.

3 Click the Zoom In button twice to a 400% view.

4 On the Paint Editor canvas, click the ball shape and then click and drag control points to sculpt the ball into a head shape.

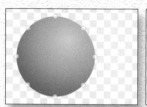  

5 Click the Ellipse tool, click the Solid option, select the black color swatch, and then click and drag to draw one of the eyes (hold the Shift key for a perfect circle).

6 Click the Duplicate tool, click the eye, and drag the copy into place.

 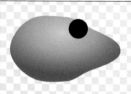 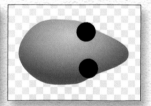

SET THE SNAKE IN MOTION

In a typical snake game, the player is always moving forward at the same speed while clicking buttons to turn left or right in pursuit of food. It's like combining the constant motion of the *Ping-Pong* ball with the left and right movement of the paddle.

MAKE THE SPRITE MOVE FORWARD

You must put the MOVE block inside a FOREVER block to create a loop that keeps the snake moving forward.

1 Click the Scripts tab for the snake sprite.

2 Drag these blocks into the Scripts Area and change the MOVE value to *2:*

ADD TURNING BLOCKS

To avoid slithering head first off the Stage, you need to add two sets of blocks to turn your snake in each direction.

1 Drag two WHEN KEY PRESSED blocks from the Events category into the Scripts Area.

2 Drag and snap a TURN block beneath each WHEN KEY PRESSED block and change the values to *90.*

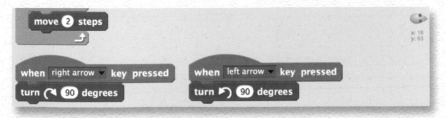

If you click the Green Flag button on the Stage, the snake moves forward on its own, turns left when you press the Left-Arrow key, and turns right when you press the Right-Arrow key.

ADD BODY TO THE SNAKE

If the head always moves at a constant speed, you can use a neat cloning trick to create body segments that follow the head around each turn.

CREATE BODY CLONING LOOP

You will need a WAIT block to slow down the creation of clones. So the next set of blocks needs to go under another WHEN GREEN FLAG CLICKED block or the new WAIT will slow down the snake movement, too.

1 Drag another WHEN GREEN FLAG CLICKED block into the Scripts Area beneath the previous blocks or to the right.

2 Drag and snap the remaining blocks pictured beneath WHEN GREEN FLAG CLICKED and change WAIT to .25.

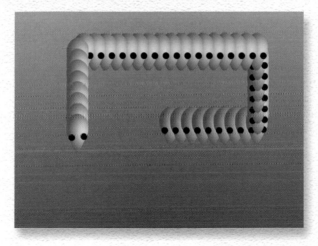

When you click the Green Flag button, the head moves the same way as before, but now a strange-looking body (made of several more *heads!?!*) trails behind.

MAKE CLONES DIFFERENT

When you create a clone of a sprite, you can use the WHEN I START AS A CLONE block to give instructions to each new clone, such as changing the size or switching costumes.

Test your code again and you have a much more suitable body shape. But since you sculpted the head, the body sections appear thicker, which looks more like a caterpillar. And the snake length appears to be endless.

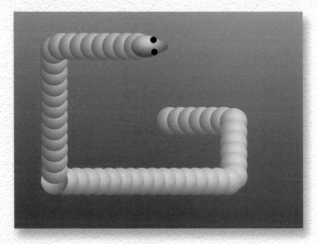

You can fix both of those problems by adding three more blocks under WHEN I START AS A CLONE. The last block might surprise you.

The SET SIZE TO block makes the body sections a bit smaller than the head. But what's up with WAIT and DELETE THIS CLONE? Click the Green Flag button and see what happens. Your snake moves the same way across the Stage, but now appears much shorter. Can you figure out why?

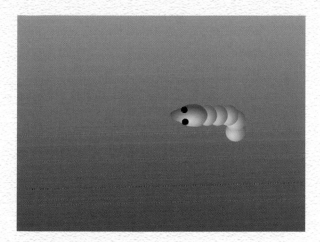

When the game starts, the head creates a clone of itself and then immediately moves two steps. But when the clone is created, it waits a quarter of a second (.25) before moving, so it's a few steps behind the head. Each clone is the same distance behind the previous one.

Change the value to WAIT 5 SECS and see what happens. You get a much longer snake, right?

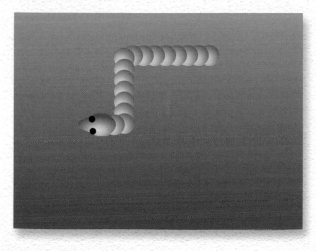

ADD FOOD FOR THE SNAKE

Each time the snake eats, the snake should grow a bit longer and another snack needs to appear somewhere else.

CREATE FOOD SPRITE

You can choose any sprite you want or paint your own food. I'll just use another ball and change the color and size.

1 Click the Choose Sprite from Library icon beneath the Stage.

2 Choose an object to act as food for the snake and then click OK.

3 Click the Info button on the sprite and change the name to *Food*.

4 Click the Costumes tab.

5 If there's more than one costume, select the one you want to use. (I'll use orange for my grub.)

6 Change the costume name to *Food1* (in case you want to add different snacks later) and then delete the other costumes.

RANDOMIZE FOOD LOCATION

Drag your food sprite to the lower-left corner of the Stage. Then use the X and Y coordinates to set the values for your random movement blocks.

1 **Drag the food sprite to the bottom-left edge of the Stage.**

2 **Click the Scripts tab.**

In the top-right corner is a faded version of the sprite with its current X and Y coordinates beneath it.

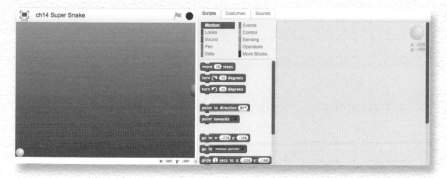

People are often confused by the X and Y coordinates that appear right below the Stage. Those are not for the sprite; they are the position of the cursor on the Stage.

3 **Drag WHEN GREEN FLAG CLICKED and GO TO X Y blocks into the Scripts Area.**

4 **Drag two PICK RANDOM # blocks into the two GO TO slots.**

5 **Use the X value and Y values from your food's position on the bottom-left corner for your random range. (Scratch will pick a number between the negative and positive values.)**

Click the Green Flag button several times and the food sprite should appear in a different location each time.

SET UP GAME COLLISIONS

In the *Ping-Pong* game, *Sensing* category blocks detect when a ball hits a paddle and the ball bounces when it hits the edge of the Stage. This game will check whether the snake head collides with the food, the edge of the screen, or its own body. (That's right. You're not even allowed to touch *yourself* in this game!)

CHECK FOR SNAKE AND SNACK COLLISION

1 Click the *Food* icon beneath the Stage and click the Scripts tab.

2 Shift-click (or right-click) the GO TO X Y block, choose *Duplicate,* and drag the copy off to the side. (You will use the copy to move the food if collision is detected.)

3 Drag and snap these blocks beneath the GO TO X Y block:

```
go to x: pick random -228 to 228 y: pick random -168 to 168
forever
    if  touching color ■ ?  then
                                    go to x: pick random -228 to 228 y: pi
```

4 Click inside the TOUCHING COLOR block and then click one of the snake's eyes.

5 Drag and snap the copied GO TO X Y block into the IF THEN block.

```
go to x: pick random -228 to 228  y: pick random -168 to 168
forever
    if      touching color ■ ?  then
        go to x: pick random -228 to 228  y: pick random -168 to 168
```

Click the Green Flag button and steer your snake toward the food. Each time the head collides with the food, the food should instantly move to another location.

MAKE THE EDGE OF THE STAGE DEADLY

In the *Ping-Pong* game, the ball bounces off the sides of the Stage because of the IF ON EDGE, BOUNCE block. But you don't want the snake to *bounce;* you want it to *die!* So you need a different *Sensing* category block here.

1 **Click the snake icon beneath the Stage and click the Scripts tab.**

2 **Instead of adding another FOREVER block, you can snap the TOUCHING block inside the FOREVER block that's already there beneath MOVE 2 STEPS.**

```
when     clicked
forever
    move 2 steps
    if      touching edge ▼ ?  then
        stop all ▼
```
x: 201
y: 37

3 Make sure the TOUCHING block's value is *Edge*.

4 Click the Green Flag button to test your code.

When you steer your serpent to the edge of the screen, the game stops. The other event that ends the game is the head running into its tail, as if it is a poisonous snake that bites itself.

MAKE THE SNAKE'S BODY DEADLY

How do you check for a collision between the head and the body if they are the same sprite? Since that costume does not have any black in it, you can use the same *Sensing* category block you used to detect the food.

1 Click the snake icon beneath the Stage and click the Scripts tab.

2 Drag another WHEN I START AS A CLONE block into the Scripts Area (beside or beneath the other blocks).

3 Drag and snap these remaining blocks beneath it:

Test your code. I bet the snake starts to move and then the entire program stops within one second. Can you figure out why?

DELAY BODY COLLISION

You need to add a WAIT block to the second WHEN I START AS A CLONE set of blocks. Be careful where you snap it in or you might throw off your head-to-body collision.

Set the value of the WAIT block to *1* SECS and test your game again. Each clone waits just long enough to be behind where the eyes are on the head and your snake slinks around until the head runs back into the tail. You may need to increase the WAIT time, depending on the size of your sprite costumes and the speed the player is moving.

Oops, I spotted a few problems that mess up the head-to-body collision in my game.

TROUBLESHOOT SNAKE COLLISION

If the snake's head is touching the edge of the Stage at the beginning of the game, the game ends right away. And because the eyes are on the side of the head, they may touch the side of a body clone in a tight turn.

An easy fix for the first problem is to set the snake's position at the beginning of the game. Go to the first WHEN GREEN FLAG CLICKED block and add a GO TO X Y block <u>before</u> the FOREVER block that keeps the snake moving.

```
when    clicked                                          x: -85
                                                          y: 159
go to x: 0 y: 0
forever
    move 2 steps
```

As for the eyes, you can either move them closer together in the Paint Editor or make the body a bit smaller. I think the second solution is better because my snake still looks a bit too much like a centipede (which is an *entirely* different game). The body size is set to 75%. I'm going to try 50%.

```
 clicked          when I start as a clone      when I start as a clone      x: -108
                                                                             y: 126
                  switch costume to body       wait 1 secs
25 secs          set size to 50 %             forever
one of myself     wait 5 secs                     if    touching color ■ ? th
```

Now when I move the snake around, the eye collision is working. Best of all, the smaller body sections make it look more snakelike.

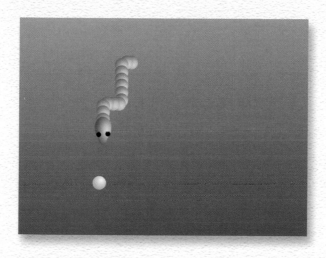

CODE SNAKE GROWTH

In your snake scripts, can you find what determines how long the snake is? Look under the first WHEN I START AS A CLONE block. That WAIT block value makes the snake shorter or longer, right? Try changing it to *8* seconds and testing your game. Then try *2* seconds.

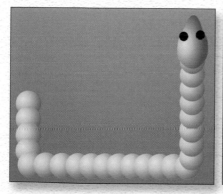

You need to increase that value each time the snake eats. Instead of using a *set value* (a number that doesn't change) inside the WAIT block, you should use a *variable,* which you can increase each time the snake collides with the food.

CREATE THE SNAKE'S LENGTH VARIABLE

1 Beneath the Scripts tab, click the *Data* category.

2 Click the Make a Variable button, type Length, choose *For All Sprites,* and click OK.

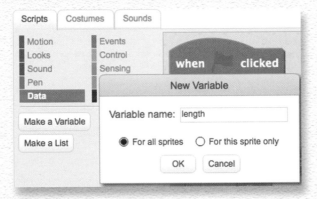

3 Drag and snap a SET TO block beneath the first WHEN GREEN FLAG CLICKED block and make sure the value is *2.* (This begins the game with a short snake.)

4 Drag a LENGTH variable into the WAIT block beneath WHEN I START AS A CLONE.

If you click the Green Flag button, your snake begins with a short length. The LENGTH variable also appears on the top-left corner of the Stage. You will eventually want to hide the variable from players, but it can be useful to display while completing your scripting.

CONTROL THE SNAKE'S LENGTH WITH CODE

What causes the snake to grow longer? Eating! All you need to do is add a CHANGE LENGTH BY block to grow the snake.

1 Click the *Food* icon beneath the Stage and click the Scripts tab.

2 Drag a CHANGE LENGTH BY block to snap between the IF THEN block and GO TO X Y. Leave the initial value of 1 for now.

When you start the game, the snake starts short but should now grow longer each time it eats a snack.

TRACK PLAYER SCORE

You can use Scratch's built-in timer to increase the score throughout the game. With the snake length working, you can hide that variable to make room for a new score variable.

HIDE THE LENGTH VARIABLE

1 Click the snake icon beneath the Stage.

2 On the Scripts tab, click the *Data* category.

3 Uncheck the *Length* variable box to hide it behind the Stage.

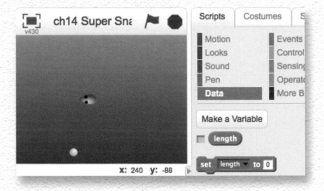

CREATE THE PLAYER'S SCORE VARIABLE

1 Beneath the Scripts tab, click the *Data* category.

2 Click the Make a Variable button, type Score, choose *For All Sprites,* and click OK.

3 Drag the Score display into position on the Stage.

4 **Drag the following blocks into the snake sprite's Scripts Area:**

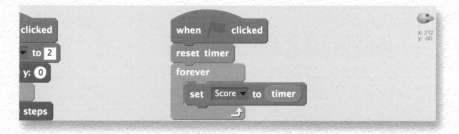

In Scratch, the timer is always running, so you need to be sure you include a RESET TIMER block so the score starts over at the beginning of each game.

It's that time, my Scratch Friend. Click that beautiful Green Flag button and test your COMPLETED SUPER SNAKE GAME!

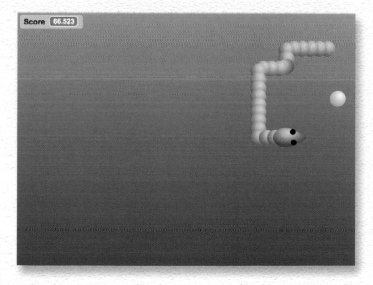

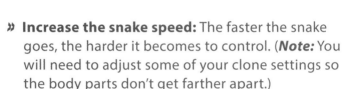

WAYS TO MAKE SUPER SNAKE MORE CHALLENGING

Though it should already be fun to play, you may want to make the game tougher for your friends. Here are some quick solutions.

» **Increase the snake speed:** The faster the snake goes, the harder it becomes to control. (**Note:** You will need to adjust some of your clone settings so the body parts don't get farther apart.)

» **Decrease size of food:** You could do this at the beginning of the game or have the size decrease as the game progresses.

» **Increase the pause between turns:** You used a WAIT block to keep the player from turning around and around. You can increase the WAIT value to make turning exactly when a player wants to even more.

» **Add baby snakes:** Once the snake reaches a certain length, or if it eats the wrong snack, you could have a small part split off and become another snake. If the player touches the new snake, it's lights out.

» **Rig the game:** If you want to be really sneaky, you could place the snacks right on the edge of the Stage at set intervals.

PROJECT 3 A-MAZE-ING GAME

WHILE PONG IS THE FIRST VIDEOGAME I EVER PLAYED, PAC-MAN IS THE ONLY GAME I EVER SAW MY GRANDMOTHER PLAYING! Maybe that explains why it became the highest grossing game in history. (More than ten billion quarters. You do the math!)

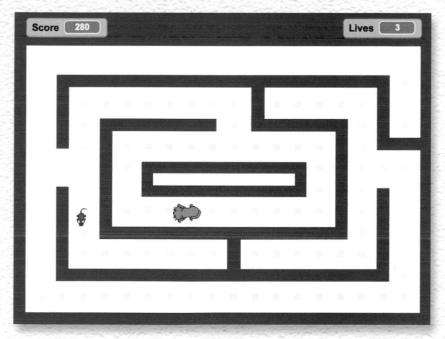

CREATE A NEW PROJECT

1 Go to scratch.mit.edu or open the Scratch 2 Offline Editor.

2 If you are online, click Create. If offline, select File ⇨ New.

3 Rename your project. (If online, select the title and type Amazing Mouse. **If using the offline version of Scratch, select File ⇨ Save As and type** Amazing Mouse.)

4 Delete the cat with the Scissors (or Shift-click the cat and choose *Delete*).

CHOOSE GAME CHARACTERS

Before drawing your maze, having all your character sprites on the Stage is helpful. Then you can design a maze in which they can fit into.

1 Beneath the Stage, click the Choose Sprite from Library icon.

2 Choose the *Animals* category.

3 Double-click the sprite named *Mouse1*.

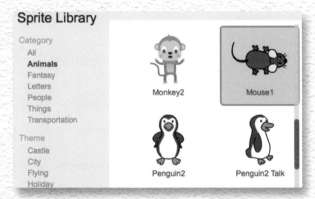

4 Repeat Steps 1–3 but choose the sprite named *Cat2*.

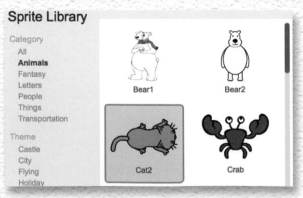

RESIZE CHARACTERS WITH CODE

Because the cat will be the larger sprite, find the right size for that character first.

1 Click the cat sprite and then click the Scripts tab.

2 Drag the WHEN GREEN FLAG CLICKED block and the SET SIZE TO block into the Scripts Area and snap them together.

3 Change the value to 30 inside the SET SIZE TO block.

4 Click the SET SIZE TO block to resize the cat sprite.

COPY BLOCKS BETWEEN SPRITES

The mouse needs the same blocks you just created. Here's a quick way to copy them over.

1 Drag the WHEN GREEN FLAG CLICKED block from the cat Scripts Area to the mouse sprite.

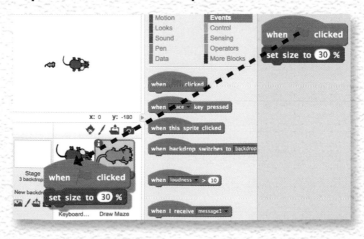

2 Click the mouse sprite and make sure the code copied over.

3 Change the value of SET SIZE TO from *30* to *20*.

4 Click the SET SIZE TO block once to resize the mouse sprite.

If you compare the cat and mouse sizes on the Stage, they should look proportionate now. So onto maze building!

DESIGN MAZE BACKGROUND

Remember in *Pac-Man* having to eat little dots before getting to the next level? I want to have little bits of cheese for the mouse to munch all the way around the maze.

Lining up all those bits inside your maze could be tricky, though, so what if we place the bits first and then use them as a guide to help draw the maze walls?

1 Beneath the Stage, click the Paint New Sprite icon.

2 Click the Costumes tab.

3 Click the Zoom In button (plus sign) four times to get to 1600%.

4 Click the Brush tool.

5 Drag the Line Width slider to the middle.

6 Click a yellow color swatch.

7 Click the middle of the Paint Editor canvas one time.

8 Shift-click the new sprite, choose *Info,* change the name to *Cheese,* and click the Back button to close the Info window.

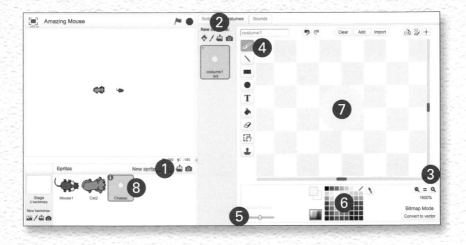

PLACE ROWS OF CHEESE USING CLONE BLOCKS

Cloning enables you to create up to 300 copies of a sprite. Each clone includes the scripts, costumes, sounds, and properties of the original sprite (which is referred to as the *parent* of the clone or clones).

1 **Click the Scripts tab of *Cheese*.**

2 **Drag the following code blocks into the Scripts Area and change the values to match:**

```
when      clicked                                    x: 240
                                                     y: 170
go to x: -230 y: 170
repeat 20
    create clone of myself ▼
    move 24 steps
```

If you click the Green Flag button to test your code, you should see one row of cheese drawn across the top of the Stage.

That 21st piece on the right side of the Stage is the original piece, so you have 20 clones and 1 original. Eventually, you will hide the original.

FILL THE STAGE WITH CHEESE BITS

1 Drag and snap a SET X TO block and a CHANGE Y BY block to the bottom of the REPEAT 20 block.

2 Change the SET X TO value to *-230* and the CHANGE Y BY value to *-24*.

3 Drag and snap another REPEAT block between the GO TO X Y and REPEAT 20 blocks.

Notice how the REPEAT block wraps around the REPEAT 20 and the GO TO and CHANGE Y blocks beneath it.

4 Change the value of the new REPEAT block to *15*.

```
when      clicked

go to x: -230 y: 170
repeat 15
    repeat 20
        create clone of myself ▾
        move 24 steps
    set x to -230
    change y by -24
```

Now, when you click the Green Flag button, the entire Stage should be filled with cheese (every mouse's dream).

To hide the original cheese sprite, you can add a HIDE block to the bottom of your code. But, because the clones need to be created each time you run your code, you will need a SHOW block at the beginning of your code. Here's what the final cheese cloning code should look like:

```
when [ ] clicked
show
go to x: -230 y: 170
repeat 15
    repeat 20
        create clone of myself ▾
        move 24 steps
    set x to -230
    change y by -24
hide
```

Scratch only allows you to create 300 clones, so I went with 15 rows and 20 columns (15 × 20 = 300).

The cloned cheese sprites will now serve as a grid to help you place the walls of the maze.

CREATE MAZE WALLS

I recently stumbled onto this quick and easy way using a series of rectangles in Vector Mode.

1 **If the cheesy grid is no longer on the Stage, click the Green Flag button to draw the clones again.**

2 **Click the Stage button beneath the actual Stage, to the left of your sprites.**

3 **Click the Backdrops tab.**

 4 **Click the Convert to Vector button.**

5 **Click the Rectangle tool.**

6 **Click the Outline option button.**

7 **Drag the Line Width slider all the way to the right for maximum line thickness.**

8 **Click the color swatch you wish to use for the walls. (I will use a dark blue.)**

9 **Click the = sign between the Zoom In and Zoom Out buttons to zoom back to 100%.**

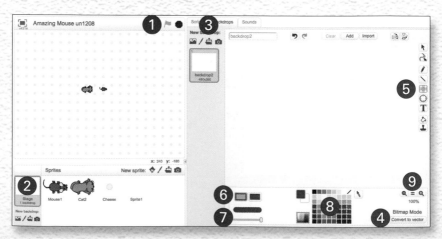

Draw a rectangle on the Paint Editor canvas and then resize it (by clicking and dragging the edge points). The first rectangle should intersect the left, right, and bottom dots. Skip the first line of dots to leave room to display the score and lives information for the player.

Draw three more rectangles and adjust the sides so each is centered over a row or column of cheesy dots.

It's important to provide enough space between all your walls for your sprites to move and in the corners for them to turn around.

CUT THROUGH MAZE WALLS

You could cut holes in the walls using the Reshape tool, but I have an even better solution. Instead of blue rectangles, why not draw solid white rectangles over the blue walls?

1 **Click the Rectangle tool.**

2 **Choose the Solid option and the white color swatch.**

3 Click and drag a small rectangle over one of the blue walls.

4 Check the position of the new "hole" on the Stage and adjust the position to fit directly over a yellow dot. (You can nudge the selected rectangle by clicking the Left- or Right-Arrow keys on your keyboard.)

DUPLICATE WALL OPENINGS

You can quickly place several wall openings by using the Duplicate tool.

1 Click the Duplicate tool.

2 Hold the Shift key on your keyboard.

3 Click the white rectangle and drag to another location, and another, and another.

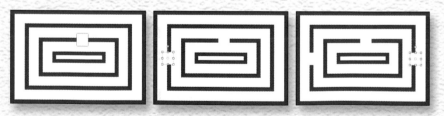

4 Adjust the position of each wall opening on the Paint Editor canvas to line up with yellow dots on the Stage.

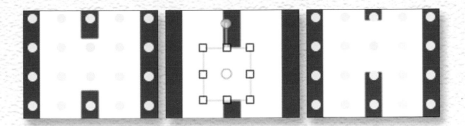

COMPLICATE THE MAZE WITH DEAD ENDS

Instead of the Rectangle tool, use the Line tool to draw a few extra walls.

1 On the Paint Editor canvas, click the Line tool.

2 Choose the same color and line thickness you chose for the rectangles.

3 In a few locations, click and drag from one wall to another to create dead ends.

4 Check the Stage and adjust the line position to intersect the yellow dots.

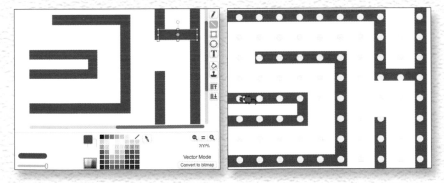

It may help to drag your mouse and cat where you want them to start on the Stage (between walls and not facing dead ends) so you can make sure you do not accidentally trap them.

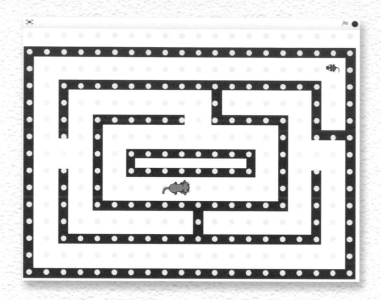

REMOVE CHEESE INSIDE WALLS

Another useful thing about clones is you can give them instructions to carry out as soon as they are created by using the WHEN I START AS A CLONE block.

1 **Click the cheesy sprite.**

2 **Click the Scripts tab.**

3 **Drag these blocks into the Scripts Area until they snap together.**

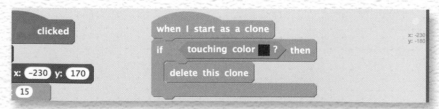

4 **Click the small color swatch inside the IF TOUCHING COLOR block, move your cursor over to the Stage, and click your wall to select the exact same color.**

If you click the Green Flag, the clones will start filling the screen, but now any cheese touching a wall disappears.

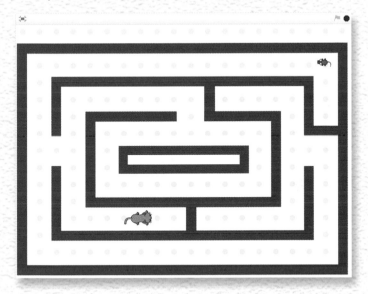

Now what's the easy way to get rid of those dots across the top of the screen? Fill it with a rectangle the same color as your walls!

With your maze walls and cheese in place, you are ready to add movement to your game characters.

ADD PLAYER KEYBOARD CONTROLS

I called my game *Amazing Mouse,* so the player will control the mouse by using the arrow keys on the keyboard. I prefer to use the KEY PRESSED? block in the *Sensing* category because it gives smoother movement than the WHEN KEY PRESSED block used in the previous project.

1 **On the Stage, click the mouse sprite and drag it to a good starting position between walls and not too close to the player.**

2 **Click the Scripts tab and the *Motion* category.**

3 **Drag and snap a GO TO X Y block to the bottom of the SET SIZE TO block in the Scripts Area. Because the mouse is the last sprite moved on the Stage, X and Y will be its current position.**

4 **Drag and snap the rest of these blocks to the bottom of the GO TO X Y block and change the values inside the blocks to match those in the image:**

Click the Green Flag button to test your new code. When you click the Right-Arrow key on your keyboard, the player sprite (*Mouse1* in my game) should move smoothly to the right.

DUPLICATE CODE BLOCKS

You will need the same blocks to check for the other three arrow keys (left, up, and down). Let's duplicate the blocks to save time.

1 **Shift-click the IF THEN block and choose *Duplicate*.**

2 **Drag the copied blocks down to snap beneath the previous IF THEN block, making sure they are still inside the FOREVER loop.**

3 **Change KEY PRESSED to *Left Arrow* and POINT IN DIRECTION to *-90*.**

4 **Repeat Steps 1-3 for *Up Arrow* and *Down Arrow*.**

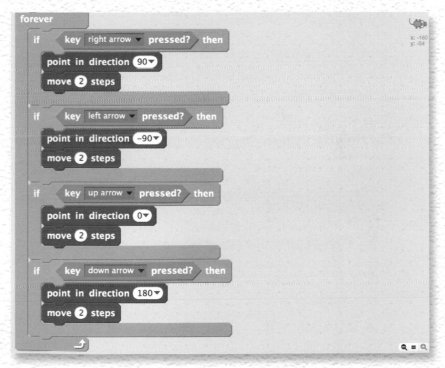

Click the Green Flag button to test your code, and you will find the arrow keys now move the sprite in all four directions, but it will pass right through walls.

MAKE WALLS STOP THE MOUSE

The same way you used the wall color to delete unwanted cheese clones, you can check to see whether the mouse is touching walls.

1 Drag these blocks into the Scripts Area for the mouse sprite:

2 Click the color swatch inside the IF TOUCHING COLOR block and then click anywhere on the wall over on the Stage.

3 Set the MOVE block to –2.

4 Click the Green Flag to test your new code.

You should be able to control your mouse movement with the arrow keys the same as before, but when it gets to a wall it should stop in place.

THE MOUSE EATS THE CHEESE

If the mouse and the clone are colliding with each other, which sprite should you put the code on to delete the clone? On the cheese!

1 Click the Cheese sprite beneath the Stage and then click the Scripts tab.

2 Drag and snap a FOREVER block to the bottom of the blocks connected to WHEN I START AS A CLONE.

3 Drag these blocks over to snap into the FOREVER block and change TOUCHING to *Mouse1*.

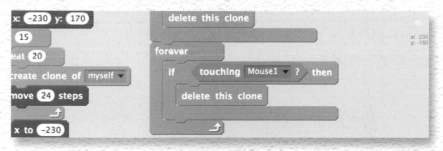

After clicking the Green Flag button, you should find each cheesy clone disappears as soon as the mouse scurries over it.

CONNECT SCORE TO SNACKING

You will need to create a variable to keep track of the score and then add code blocks to increase the score with each cheese chomp.

1 Beneath the Scripts tab, click the *Data* category.

2 Click the Make a Variable button and type Score, **leave** *For All Sprites* **selected, and then click OK.**

3 Drag and snap a SET TO block to the bottom of the WHEN GREEN FLAG CLICKED block in the Scripts Area and make sure the Score value is *0*.

4 Drag and snap a CHANGE SCORE BY block between IF TOUCHING MOUSE1 and DELETE THIS CLONE.

5 Set the CHANGE SCORE BY value to the amount each piece of cheese is worth. (I'll use 10.)

6 On the Stage, you can drag the *Score* display to reposition it.

When you click the Green Flag and move through the maze, the bits of cheese should disappear and the score should increase.

But, how do you keep track of the number of cheese bits eaten?

KEEP TRACK OF THE CHEESE LEFT

What if you create another variable, set it to 300 at the beginning, and then subtract one each time a clone is deleted?

1 Create another variable named *Cheese*. (Follow Steps 1–3 in the previous section.)

2 On the Stage, drag the *Cheese* display to the top-right corner. (You will hide it after confirming the cheese counter code works. Try saying that five times in a row!)

3 Drag and snap a SET TO block beneath SET SCORE TO in the Scripts Area. Change the value to 300 and make sure the *Cheese* value is selected.

```
when     clicked          when I start as a clone

set  Score ▼  to 0        if    touching color ■ ?  then       x: -230
                                                               y: -180
set  Cheese ▼  to 300         delete this clone

show
```

4 Drag and snap a CHANGE BY block to the top of each DELETE THIS CLONE block and set the values to *Cheese* and *–1*.

```
ore ▼  to 0               if    touching color ■ ?  then

eese ▼  to 300                change  Cheese ▼  by -1          x: -230
                                                               y: -180
x: -230  y: 170               delete this clone

15                        forever

at 20                         if    touching  Mouse1 ▼  ?  then

reate clone of  myself ▼          change  Score ▼  by 10

ove 24 steps                      change  Cheese ▼  by -1

                                  delete this clone
```

As soon as a DELETE THIS CLONE block runs, no other code on that code can execute. That's why you must snap the CHANGE CHEESE BY −1 _above_ each of these blocks.

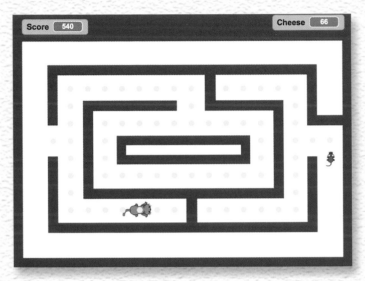

When you click the Green Flag button, the cheese counter should start at 300 but immediately decrease as clones touching the wall are deleted.

PROGRAM ENEMY PATROL

As you learn more about programming, you will be able to create more devious enemies. For now, we just need the cat to wander around the maze and take a life away from the player each time the cat and mouse collide until the player has no lives left.

GIVE THE ENEMY MARCHING ORDERS

1 **On the Stage, drag the enemy sprite (the cat in my game) into a good starting position (between walls and not too close to the player).**

2 Click the Scripts tab and then the Motion category.

3 Drag and snap a GO TO X Y block to the bottom of SET SIZE TO in the Scripts Area.

4 Drag and snap the rest of these blocks to the bottom of the GO TO X Y block and change the values inside the blocks to match those in the image. (Don't forget to select the wall color inside the TOUCHING COLOR block.)

Clicking the Green Flag button sets the size and position and the FOREVER loop starts the cat roving. You can make the enemy patrol more territory by turning 90 degrees each time it reaches a wall instead of 180 degrees.

If you find your enemy sprite just spinning around in place, there are several possible fixes. The easiest may be to adjust the sprite's starting position or make it a bit smaller. If you do not want to decrease the size of your enemy sprite further, you can either adjust the length or change the center of rotation.

ADJUST THE SPRITE LENGTH

I don't know about your enemy, but in some corners my cat gets stuck. It appears the tail is getting caught in the wall. You can avoid such problems by adjusting the length of your sprite. I need to tuck the tail in to make my cat shorter.

1 Click the Costumes tab.

2 Click the Select tool.

3 Click the tail and drag it against the body.

 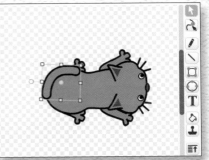

4 Click the Green Flag button to test the new shape.

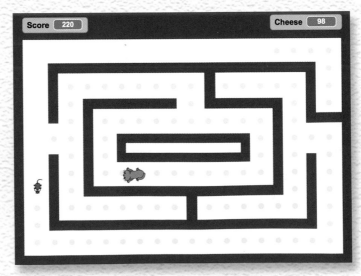

CHANGE THE CENTER OF ROTATION

If the costume center is off, when the sprite gets to a corner of your maze, it will hit a wall, turn 90 degrees, and then may still be touching a wall, so it turns again and again and again.

Here's how you can fix it:

1 Click the sprite you wish to edit and then click the Costumes tab.

2 Click the Set Costume Center button.

3 Click and drag to adjust the center of the black crosshairs over the part of your sprite that should be the center.

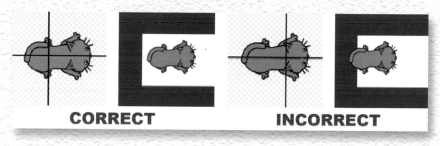

CORRECT   **INCORRECT**

TRACK PLAYER LIVES

A new variable must be created if you want to give your player more than one life.

1 Go to the Scripts tab for the player sprite. (That's *Mouse1* for me.)

2 Click Data and then click the Make a Variable button. Name the new variable *Lives* and click OK.

3 Uncheck the box next to the *Cheese* variable (as you no longer need to display this on the Stage).

4 Drag and snap a SET TO block between WHEN GREEN FLAG CLICKED and FOREVER, then change the values to match (*Lives* and *3*).

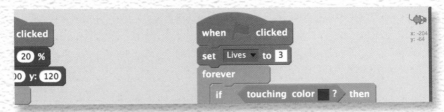

5 Beneath IF TOUCHING COLOR and MOVE −2 steps, add the blocks pictured here (another IF THEN block):

6 Change the values in the GO TO X Y block to the player's starting X and Y values.

7 To end the game when the player has no more lives left, add these blocks between CHANGE LIVES BY and GO TO X Y:

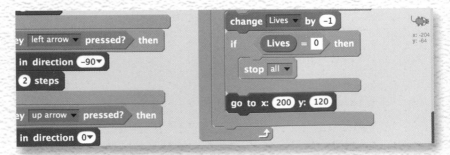

8 On the Stage, drag the Lives indicator to the top-right corner.

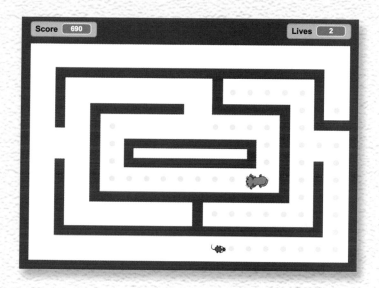

Click the Green Flag button and run right into the enemy to make sure a life is subtracted. If you touch the enemy three times, the game should end.

GIVE PLAYER A CHANCE TO WIN

You created a variable to keep track of the number of cheese bits left in the maze, but what if the player clears the maze of all the cheese? After all that scurrying about and avoiding the enemy, the player deserves SOMETHING, right?

To trigger some sort of victory sound or message once the maze is cleared, use another IF THEN block.

1 Click the enemy icon (*Cat2* for me) and then click the Sounds tab.

2 Click the Choose Sound from Library button and pick a suitable tune. (I like the one named *Triumph*.)

3 Double-click a sound to load it into your sprite.

4   Click the Scripts tab and then drag and snap an IF THEN block along with the other blocks shown into the FOREVER block above the MOVE block:

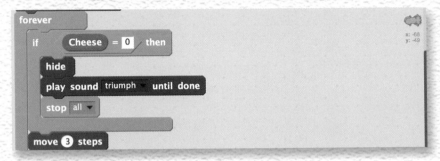

5   Whenever you add a HIDE block, it's a good idea to put a SHOW block near the beginning of your code or the enemy will not appear in the next game or level.

I chose a PLAY SOUND UNTIL DONE block for the final sound, so the *Triumph* music can finish playing before the STOP block ends all scripts.

Having only a victory sound seems kinda lame to me. Why not add sounds to the following events, too:

» Munching each cheese bit. (Add to the *Cheese* scripts.)

» Being caught by the cat. (Add to the *Mouse1* scripts.)

» Losing your last life. (Add to the *Mouse1* scripts.)

Of course, you don't have to use the same sounds I've chosen from the Sound Library. You can choose other sounds, upload sounds, or even record your own! Can you think of any other ways to customize your game?

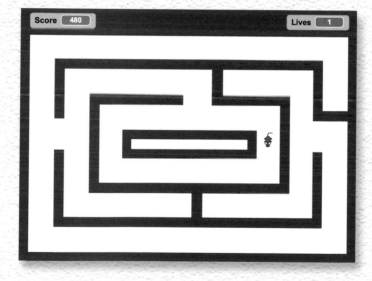

ENHANCE YOUR GAME

Here are some other ways you might improve your maze game.

» **Add more enemies:** Try duplicating your enemy sprite, starting in a different location and having it turn −90 degrees instead of 90 degrees.

» **Add additional levels:** When cheese = 0, you could to switch to another maze backdrop and repopulate the maze with cheesy clones.

» **Change enemy speed:** You could have the enemy get faster as there are fewer cheese bits left or allow the player to choose a difficulty level that speeds up the enemy, slows down the player, or both.

» **Add power-ups:** Remember in Pac-Man how the ghosts would turn blue for a few seconds after chomping one of those fat dots? You could transform the player into a dog for a few seconds to give the cat a run for its money.

PROJECT 4 ATTACKING THE CLONES

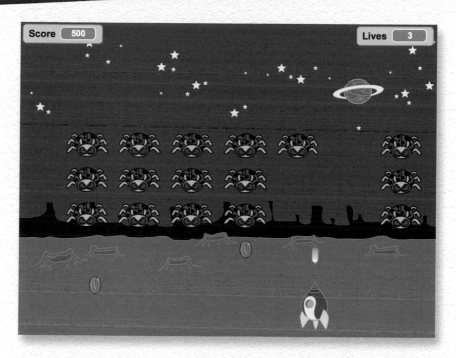

I CAN NOT IMAGINE DESIGNING A GAME LIKE THIS IN EARLIER VERSIONS OF SCRATCH, WHICH DID NOT PROVIDE A WAY TO CLONE SPRITES. While the cheese clones in Project 3 just sit in place waiting to be eaten, these clones march across the screen and fire deadly watermelon bombs! Fortunately, you can fire back with your own laser clones!

CREATE A NEW PROJECT

As always, you can name your project any way you like. I'm going to avoid the title *Space Invaders* because I *have* to (by law) and because my game is going to look much cooler!

1 Go to scratch.mit.edu or open the Scratch 2 Offline Editor.

2 If you are online, click Create. If offline, select File ⇨ New.

3 Name your project. (If online, select the title and type Space Attack. **If using the offline version of Scratch, select File ⇨ Save As and type** Space Attack.)

4 Blast that cat out of existence with the Scissors (or Shift-click the cat and choose *Delete*).

CHOOSE A GAME BACKGROUND

Although you can import a drawing or photograph or design your own backdrop on the Paint Editor canvas, let's take the easy route for a quick start: choosing one from the Backdrop Library.

 1 On the Backdrops tab, click the Choose Backdrop from Library icon.

2 Scroll to the backdrop you wish to use (I will use the one named *Space*) and double-click it.

CREATE PLAYER AND ENEMY SPRITES

You will begin with a spaceship that moves back and forth across the bottom of the screen.

1 **Beneath the Stage, click the Choose Sprite from Library icon.**

2 **Click the *Transportation* category.**

3 **Double-click the sprite named *Spaceship*.**

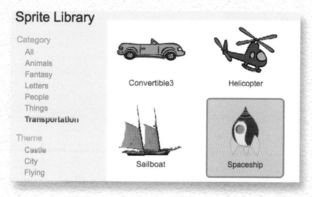

RESIZE AND POSITION THE SPACESHIP

The spaceship sprite is far too large. To resize it precisely, you will use a bit of code (rather than just using the Shrink tool). This is also a good time to set the starting position near the bottom of the screen.

1 **Click the Scripts tab.**

2 **Click, drag, and snap these blocks into the Scripts Area:**

3 Try these values: Size = *30*, X = *0*, and Y = *–140*.

4 Click the Green Flag button to test your code.

Your spaceship should now appear about a third of the size it was and be positioned in the bottom center of the Stage.

CREATE ALIEN INVADERS

No matter how many enemies you want to include in your game, thanks to clones, you only need one sprite!

 1 Beneath the Stage, click the Choose Sprite from Library icon.

2 Click the *Animals* category.

3 Double-click the sprite named *Ladybug2*.

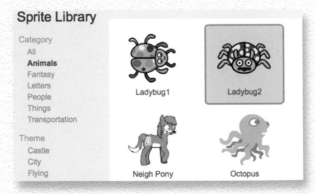

That's right. I'm going with killer ladybugs from outer space! *(Cue the terrifying space theme music.)*

I could leave the cute little bugger alone, but I think I'll make a few tweaks on the Paint Editor canvas to make it a bit more alien-looking.

MODIFY A SPRITE FROM THE SPRITE LIBRARY

 1 On the Costumes tab, click the Select tool.

 2 Click the Zoom In button to get a closer look.

3 Click the ladybug on the Paint Editor canvas to select it.

 4 Use the Color a Shape tool to change colors.

 5 Use the Reshape tool to sculpt individual shapes (like the eyes).

6 Use the Select tool to select, resize, and move shapes.

CLONE A BUNCH OF ALIENS

Instead of duplicating, you can now use a single code block to clone as many aliens as you want when the game begins. Can you see why this is so much better? You only have to make changes to that first alien and all the clones will have those changes, too. (This is called *inheriting*.)

EVENLY POSITION ALIEN CLONES

I'm getting sick of typing *ladybugalien*, so why don't you change the name of the sprite to *Alien* before adding the CREATE CLONE block.

1 **Shift-click the ladybug sprite (beneath the Stage), choose** *Info,* **and then change the name to** *Alien.*

2 **Click the white triangle button to exit** *Info.*

3 **Click the Scripts tab.**

4 **Drag the following blocks into the Scripts Area and change the values to match (you will find the CREATE CLONE block in the Control category):**

```
when      clicked
set size to 50 %
go to x: -200 y: 100
create clone of myself ▾
```

Reducing the size of the alien to 50% will allow you to fit more of them on the screen. But why can't you see the alien clone? Because the original alien and the clone are in exactly the same position!

Add a CHANGE X block, change the value to *90*, click the Green Flag button, and see what happens.

Now the original sprite (the *parent*) makes a clone of itself then moves 60 pixels to the right so you can see the two aliens side-by-side.

How do you create an entire row of aliens? Drag a REPEAT block over to surround CREATE CLONE and CHANGE X BY. Set the REPEAT value to *7* to fit the maximum number of aliens across the Stage.

If you need to change the X value by 60 to place alien clones side-by-side, what do you need to change to create additional *rows* of aliens? The Y value!

You can add another REPEAT block, but you also need to set the X value back to -200 so the parent sprite starts each row in the same location (along the left side of the Stage).

```
when [flag] clicked
set size to (50) %
go to x: (-200) y: (100)
repeat (3)
  repeat (7)
    create clone of [myself ▼]
    change x by (60)
  set x to (-200)
  change y by (-40)
```

x: 220
y: -180

Once you have all your clones lined up on the Stage (3 rows, 7 aliens across), you need to hide your parent sprite. Add a HIDE block at the end of your alien cloning code, then add a SHOW block at the beginning of the code, so each time you click the Green Flag button the original alien sprite will appear, create all the clones, and then hide during the game.

```
when [flag] clicked
show
set size to (50) %
go to x: (-200) y: (100)
repeat (3)
  repeat (7)
    create clone of [myself ▼]
    change x by (60)
  set x to (-200)
  change y by (-40)
hide
```

x: -200
y: -20

Now that you have all those aliens on the screen, how about telling them to do something?

GIVE CLONES THEIR MARCHING ORDERS

To make all your aliens march to the right at the beginning of the game, drag the following blocks to the right of the other alien code blocks and change the values to match:

```
when        clicked              when I start as a clone
                                 forever
show
                                   move 1 steps
set size to 50 %
go to x: -200 y: 100
```

When you click the Green Flag button, the aliens move to the right until there is an alien traffic jam along the side of the Stage. Click the Stop button to clear the Stage traffic.

BROADCAST MESSAGE TO TURN

In videogame design, there are many times when you'll want to send a message to several sprites (or clones) at once. In Scratch, this is called *broadcasting*.

You need your alien clones to do two things: broadcast a message if they reach the edge of the Stage (if X position is greater than 210) and change direction if they receive a broadcast (TURN 180 DEGREES). You will find the BROADCAST blocks in the *Events* category.

```
when          clicked              when I start as a clone        x: -200
                                                                  y: -20
show                               forever
set size to 50 %                       move 1 steps
go to x: -200  y: 100                  if      x position > 210    then
repeat 3                                   broadcast message1
    repeat 7
        create clone of myself         when I receive message1
        move 60 steps                  turn 180 degrees
    set x to -200
```

When you click the Green Flag button, the aliens should change direction at the same time. But they are no longer lined up in neat columns, and as soon as they change direction, they all flip upside down!?!

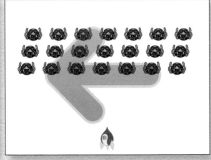

CHANGE A SPRITE'S ROTATION STYLE

If you want a sprite to point only left or right (and not look like a legs-up-dead bug), you can change the rotation from *All Around* (360 degrees) to *Left-Right* (90 degrees or –90 degrees). You also should set an initial direction so the aliens always start facing right.

1 On the alien sprite's Scripts tab, drag and snap the following blocks between WHEN GREEN FLAG CLICKED and SHOW:

```
when       clicked

set rotation style  left–right ▼

point in direction  90 ▼

show
```

2 Inside the SET ROTATION STYLE block, choose *Left-Right*.

3 Inside the POINT IN DIRECTION block, choose the direction you want the alien invaders to move first (I keep *90* or *Right*).

4 Click the Green Flag button to test the new code.

When your marching aliens reach the right side, they should now change direction without flipping upside-down. But then they get jammed up on the *left* side of the Stage.

Add the following code and change the values to broadcast a message and change direction when any alien clone reaches the *left* side of the Stage (when the X position is *less than* –210).

```
when       clicked                      when I start as a clone

set rotation style  left–right ▼         forever

point in direction  90 ▼                     move  1  steps

show                                         if    x position  > 210   then

set size to  50 %                                broadcast  message1 ▼

go to x:  -200  y:  100

repeat  3                                    if    x position  < -210   then

    repeat  7                                    broadcast  message1 ▼

        create clone of  myself ▼

        change x by  60
```

If you click the Green Flag button, those alien clones march back and forth across the Stage. But what happened to our nice, neat columns?

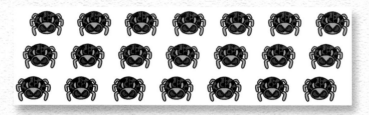

STRAIGHTEN ALIEN CLONE COLUMNS

As soon as the first alien is cloned, the code blocks under WHEN I START AS A CLONE make it move (*before* the parent is finished making all the clones). Why not have the clones wait until the last one is created by having the parent sprite send a *Start Marching* broadcast?

Before adding another broadcast message, give the first broadcast message a more descriptive name.

1 **On the enemy's Scripts tab, go to the first BROADCAST block, click *Message1,* and select *New Message.***

2 **Type *Change Direction* and then click OK.**

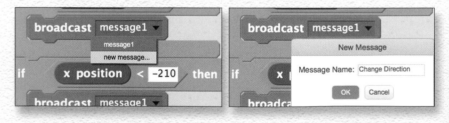

3 **In the second BROADCAST block, select *Change Direction.***

4 **Change the WHEN I RECEIVE block to *Change Direction.***

Now you can add a BROADCAST *Start Marching* block beneath the REPEAT blocks that create all the clones. Then replace the WHEN I START AS A CLONE block with WHEN I RECEIVE *Start Marching*.

1 Drag and snap a new BROADCAST MESSAGE block between the REPEAT blocks and the HIDE block in the Scripts Area.

2 In BROADCAST MESSAGE, select *New Message* and type Start Marching.

3 Drag another WHEN I RECEIVE block to the right of the WHEN I START AS A CLONE block.

4 Click and drag the FOREVER block from beneath the WHEN I START AS A CLONE block and snap it under WHEN I RECEIVE.

5 Drag the WHEN I START AS A CLONE block to the left, outside the Scripts Area to delete it.

6 Change the WHEN I RECEIVE message to *Start Marching*.

7 Click the Green Flag button to test your code.

```
when        clicked              when I receive  Start Marching ▼

set rotation style  left-right ▼    forever

point in direction  90 ▼             move  1  steps

show                                 if      x position  >  210   then

set size to  50  %                       broadcast  Change Direction ▼

go to x:  -200  y:  100

repeat  3                            if      x position  <  -210   then

    repeat  7                            broadcast  Change Direction ▼

        create clone of  myself ▼

        move  60  steps

    set x to  -200                  when I receive  Change Direction ▼

    change y by  -40                turn ↻  180  degrees

                                    change y by  -20
broadcast  Start Marching ▼

hide
```

The clones wait patiently until the final clone appears on the Stage, and then the clones should begin marching in nice, straight columns!

MAKE ALIENS MOVE DOWN, TOO

Each time the aliens reach one side, they also should move down the Stage, getting closer and closer to the player. So what do you need to add?

You don't need another broadcast message; just add a CHANGE Y block after the TURN 180 DEGREES BLOCK to make clones turn *and* drop closer to the player each time the *Change Direction* broadcast message is received.

1 **Add a CHANGE Y BY block beneath the TURN 180 DEGREES block.**

2 Set CHANGE Y BY to the amount you want enemies to get closer to the player on each turn. (I'll start with *-20*.)

3 Click the Green Flag button to test the code.

Your alien invaders should all change direction at the same time and drop down closer to the player each time they reach a side of the Stage.

ADD LASER BLASTER TO SPACESHIP

Cloning isn't just for aliens, my friends. You also can use clones to shoot them out of the sky!

CREATE A LASER SPRITE

 1 Beneath the Stage, click the Choose Sprite from Library icon.

2 Click the *Things* category and then double-click the sprite named *Button2*.

3 Shift-click the Button2 icon (beneath the Stage) and choose *Info*.

4 Change the name to *Laser*.

5 Click the Back button (white triangle in blue circle) to close the Info window.

6 Click the Costumes tab and then change the name of the first costume to *Blue* and the name of the second costume to *Orange*.

7 Click one of them to choose a starting costume. (I'll use *Orange;* I may use *Blue* later as a bonus weapon, perhaps a freeze ray!)

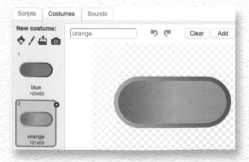

Take a moment to think about how you might transform the button to look more like a laser blast. You could modify it with the Paint tools, but I'm going to show you a shortcut.

8 Click the Scripts tab.

9 Drag these blocks into the Scripts Area and change the values to match:

```
when [flag] clicked
set size to (15) %
point in direction (0▼)
                                    x: -30
                                    y: 45
```

10 Click the SET SIZE TO block one time.

FIRE THE LASER WITH THE SPACEBAR

You can have the spaceship sprite clone the laser so it will appear to be shooting at the aliens.

1 Click the spaceship sprite's icon beneath the Stage and then click the Scripts tab.

2 Add a second set of blocks for when the player clicks the spacebar:

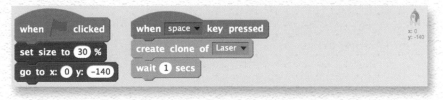

3 In the CREATE CLONE OF block, change *Myself* to *Laser*.

Each time you press the spacebar, a clone of *Laser* will be created. You can increase or decrease the value in WAIT 1 SECS to change the difficulty of the game.

One of the most important decisions you will make as a game designer is how hard your game should be. If your game is too hard, players will get frustrated and quit. And, if it's too easy, players will quickly become bored.

Before you can fire, you will need to add a bit of code to the laser sprite, too.

CREATE LASER CLONES

1 Click the laser sprite's icon beneath the Stage and then click the Scripts tab.

2 Click, drag, and snap a HIDE block to the bottom of the POINT IN DIRECTION block.

3 Drag a WHEN I START AS A CLONE block into the Scripts Area and add the blocks shown here:

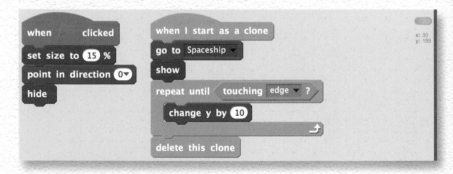

4 In the GO TO block, change *Mouse Pointer* to *Spaceship*, and set the CHANGE Y BY block's value to 10.

5 Click the Green Flag button.

When you press the spacebar, a laser clone should appear, move from the spaceship to the top of the screen, and disappear when it touches the top edge of the Stage. (I'll switch back to a white backdrop for now to make spotting the laser easier.)

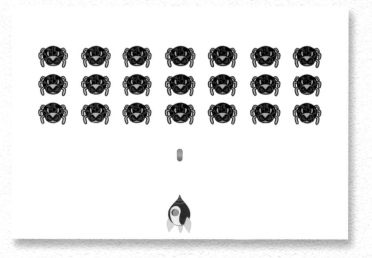

ENABLE SPACESHIP MOVEMENT

1 Click the spaceship's icon beneath the Stage and then click the Scripts tab.

2 Drag and snap a FOREVER block to the bottom of the GO TO X Y block, drag the remaining blocks below into the FOREVER block, and change the values to match:

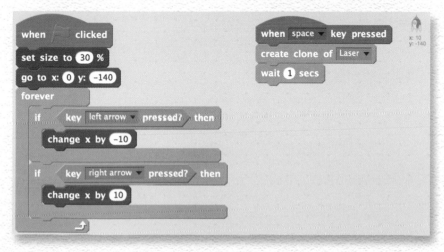

3 Click the Green Flag button to test your code.

When you press the Left- and Right-Arrow keys on your keyboard, the spaceship should move smoothly left and right. You can adjust the player movement speed by increasing or decreasing the CHANGE X BY value.

USE COLLISION TO DESTROY ALIENS

Instead of the laser passing right through the aliens as if they were ladybug-shaped clouds, you want to destroy them, right?

1 **Click the alien sprite and then click the Scripts tab.**

2 **Drag the highlighted blocks into the FOREVER block.**

3 **Click inside the IF TOUCHING block and choose *Laser*.**

4 **Click the Green Flag button to test your game.**

When you click the spacebar, a laser should shoot out of your spaceship and destroy any aliens it hits.

DELETE THE LASER ON IMPACT

When a clone of the laser is created, it will move up until it touches the edge of the screen. You can use an OR block to check whether it is touching the edge *or* touching an alien, and then delete the laser in either case.

1 Click the laser sprite and locate the REPEAT UNTIL block under the stack with the WHEN I START AS A CLONE block.

2 Drag an OR block into the laser sprite's Scripts Area. (The OR block resides in the *Operators* category.)

3 Drag a new TOUCHING block into the first OR slot and change the value to *Alien*.

4 Drag a TOUCHING block into the second OR slot and make sure the value is *Edge*.

5 Drag the OR block into the REPEAT UNTIL block, replacing the previous contents.

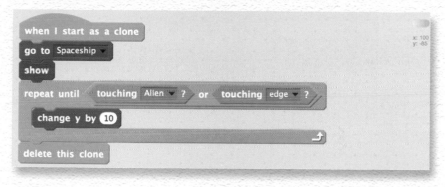

Each alien clone disappears before the laser has time to detect it has collided. The easy way to fix this is to add a slight time delay between when a laser hits an alien and when the alien clone is deleted.

1 Go to the allen sprite's Scripts tab.

2 Drag and snap a WAIT block to the top of the DELETE THIS CLONE block.

3 Change the WAIT value to *.01*.

4 Click the Green Flag button to test your updated laser blasting.

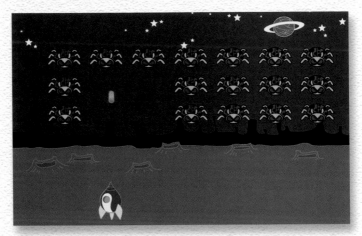

At last! Each laser should now destroy just one alien or disappear when it reaches the top edge of the Stage.

If your laser moves too far on each move, it might not collide with the enemy. So, if lasers are still passing right through aliens, try lowering the MOVE value. (A value of 20 was too much for my game, but 10 worked well.)

PROGRAM ENEMIES TO DROP BOMBS

You can use the same cloning technique to have aliens attack the player, but it will require a bit more programming to have different enemies attack at random.

CREATE AN ENEMY BOMB SPRITE

I found the *perfect* sprite for our alien bug bombs!

1 Beneath the Stage, click the Choose Sprite from Library icon.

2 Click the *Things* category and then double-click the *Watermelon* sprite.

3 Shift-click the *Watermelon* sprite and choose *Info*.

4 Change the name to *Bomb*.

5 Click the Back button to close the Info window.

6 Click the Scripts tab and drag the following blocks into the Scripts Area and change the values to match:

```
when         clicked
                                                    x: 86
                                                    y: 11
point in direction 180▾
set size to 25 %
```

RANDOMIZE ENEMY ATTACKS

Can you figure out how the PICK RANDOM block (in the *Operators* category) might help randomize when a clone drops a bomb? What if you combine it with a WAIT block?

1 Click the alien sprite and then click the Scripts tab.

2 Drag an additional WHEN I RECEIVE block to the right of WHEN I RECEIVE *Start Marching* and choose *Start Marching* for this additional block, too.

3 Drag the other blocks pictured to the bottom of the new WHEN I RECEIVE block and change the values to match.

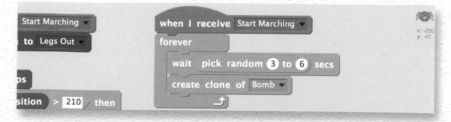

Every three to six seconds, each alien will clone a bomb. Now you need to add code to the bombs to enable them to drop toward the bottom of the Stage.

1 Click the *Bomb* sprite and click the Scripts tab.

2 Drag a WHEN I START AS A CLONE block to the right of the WHEN GREEN FLAG CLICKED block in the Scripts Area.

3 Snap the blocks pictured to the bottom of the WHEN I START AS A CLONE block and change the values to match.

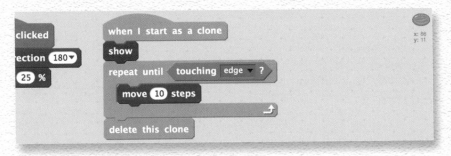

Next, you need to instruct the bombs *where* to fall *from*. You can have each alien clone tell the bomb where it is by using variables.

1 On the Scripts tab, click the *Data* category.

2 Click the Make a Variable button.

3 Change the variable name to *bomb x* (for the x position) and then click OK.

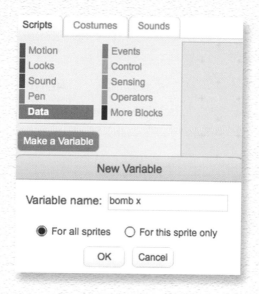

4 Make another variable named *Bomb y* (for the y position).

5 On the alien sprite's Scripts tab, add the following blocks under CREATE CLONE OF BOMB:

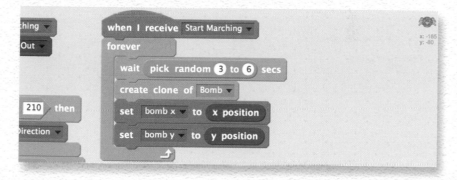

6 On the bomb sprite's Scripts tab, add a GO TO block under WHEN I START AS A CLONE and drag BOMB X and BOMB Y blocks from the *Data* category into the X and Y slots:

```
clicked                 when I start as a clone
rection  180▾           go to x:  bomb x   y:  bomb y
    25  %               show
                        repeat until   touching  edge ▾ ?
                            move  10  steps

                        delete this clone
```

Click the Green Flag button to test your game; the bomb now drops from random enemies. If your code works, GREAT JOB, because that's some tricky Scratching! If the bombs are not working for you, don't be discouraged. Double-check the preceding images to make sure you have all the blocks *and* have the correct values or settings for each block.

HIDE VARIABLES ON THE STAGE

I assume you do not want to have your *Bomb x* and *Bomb y* variables showing on the Stage during your game. I sure don't! To hide them, pull two HIDE VARIABLE blocks over to the bomb's Scripts tab, choose *Bomb x* in the first and *Bomb y* in the second block.

```
when        clicked
point in direction  180▾
set size to  25  %
hide
hide variable  bomb y ▾
hide variable  bomb x ▾
```

ADD SOUND TO YOUR GAME

Have you ever played a videogame with the sound turned off? NO THANK YOU! Sound effects are a vital part of the gaming experience, and Scratch makes adding them to your project simple. Although you can import custom sounds or record them inside Scratch, I'll stick to sounds you can find in the Sound Library.

MAKE LASERS A BLAST

You need only one block to play a sound in your Scratch project. If you want players to hear a sound each time they fire a laser at the aliens, where should that sound block go?

1 Click the spaceship sprite beneath the Stage and click the Sounds tab.

2 Click the Choose Sound from Library button.

3 Click the *Electronic* category and then double-click *Laser1* (or choose your favorite laser blaster sound).

4 Click the Scripts tab.

5 Drag and snap the PLAY SOUND block to the bottom of the CREATE CLONE OF Laser block.

6 Press the spacebar on your keyboard.

```
when space ▼ key pressed
create clone of Laser ▼
play sound laser1 ▼
wait 1 secs
```
x: 100
y: -140

As soon as you hit the spacebar, you should hear your laser blast. What sound should we add next? How about a little explosion each time you hit one of the alien invaders?

PLAY SOUND WHEN AN ALIEN IS HIT

1 Click the alien sprite beneath the Stage and click the Sounds tab.

2 Click the Choose Sound from Library button.

3 Click the Electronic category and then double-click *Screech*.

4 Click the Scripts tab.

5 Drag and snap the PLAY SOUND block to the bottom of the IF TOUCHING *Laser* THEN block.

6 Click the Green Flag button to test your game.

```
if       touching Laser ▼ ?    then
    play sound screech ▼
    wait .01 secs
    delete this clone
```
x: -177
y: -40

You should now hear the sound effect you chose (or the freaky screech I went with). See what a difference a few sound effects can make?

Now, let's give the remaining aliens a bit of satisfaction by allowing them to destroy the player!

GIVE THE PLAYER THREE LIVES

Although the average cat may get nine lives, the original *Space Invaders* only gave me three! For your game, you can grant the player as many lives as you want. Anything more than one life requires another variable to track and show the number of lives a player has left.

CREATE A VARIABLE TO TRACK PLAYER LIVES

1 On the Scripts tab, click the *Data* category.

2 Click the Make a Variable button.

3 Change the variable name to *Lives.*

4 On the spaceship sprite's Scripts tab, add another WHEN GREEN FLAG CLICKED along with the other pictured blocks and change the values to match:

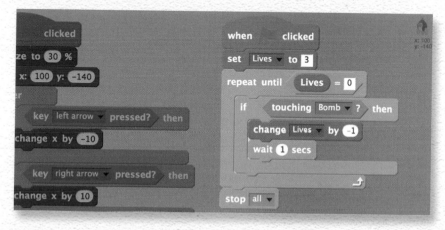

At this point, the player starts with three lives and each time an enemy bomb collides with the spaceship, the player loses one life.

Now how about some explosions to liven things up?

DESTROY A PLAYER ON IMPACT

If you play the game now, a bomb hitting the player will subtract a life, but you do not see or hear anything when that happens. Choose an appropriate sound effect and then design a new costume that looks like a puff of smoke.

PLAY SOUND WHEN THE PLAYER IS HIT

1 Click the spaceship sprite beneath the Stage and click the Sounds tab.

2 Click the Choose Sound from Library button.

3 Click the *Percussion* category and then double-click *Cymbal*.

4 Click the Scripts tab.

5 Drag and snap the PLAY SOUND block to the bottom of the IF TOUCHING BOMB THEN block.

When any bomb collides with a spaceship, you should hear the explosion sound.

ANIMATE THE PLAYER EXPLOSION

A quick way to create an explosion is to paint a new costume for the spaceship that looks like a puff of smoke.

1 Click the spaceship's Costumes tab.

2 Shift-click the first costume, choose *Duplicate,* and name the new costume *Explode.*

3 Click the Ellipse tool, choose the Solid option, and then click a medium gray color swatch.

4 Click and drag to draw several circles over the spaceship image.

5 Click the Select tool, click the spaceship, and then click the Delete key on your keyboard.

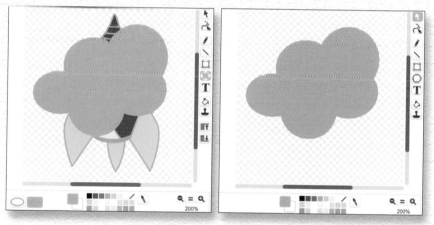

6 Click the Scripts tab.

7 Drag the following highlighted blocks into place and change the values to match:

```
clicked                          when        clicked
ze to  30  %                     set   Lives ▼ to  3
x:  100  y:  -140                repeat until    Lives  =  0
r                                  switch costume to  spaceship-a ▼
  key  left arrow ▼  pressed?  then    if      touching  Bomb ▼  ?   then
hange x by  -10                      play sound  cymbal
                                     change  Lives ▼  by  -1
  key  right arrow ▼  pressed?  then  switch costume to  explode ▼
hange x by  10                       wait  1  secs
    ↻
                                          ↻
                                 stop  all ▼
```

If you click the Green Flag button, whenever the player is hit by
a bomb, the costume should switch to the smoke cloud for 1
second and then switch back to the spaceship costume.

KEEPING SCORE

First, you must add code to the Spaceship to set the Score to 0 at
the beginning of each game.

1 **Choose the *Data* category on the spaceship's Scripts tab.**

2 **Click the Make a Variable button, name it *Score,* and then
click OK.**

3 **Drag and snap a SET SCORE TO block beneath SET LIVES
and keep the default value of *0.***

```
clicked                          when        clicked
ze to  30  %                     set   Lives ▼ to  3
x:  100  y:  -140                set   Score ▼ to  0
```

Since the score will increase each time an enemy is destroyed, you will set the code to increase the score on the alien sprite.

1 **Go to the Scripts tab for the alien sprite.**

2 **Drag and snap a CHANGE SCORE BY block between the IF TOUCHING LASER THEN block and the PLAY SOUND SCREECH block.**

3 **Set the CHANGE SCORE BY value to *100* (or whatever value you want to assign to each destroyed enemy).**

4 **Click the Green Flag button to test your game.**

The score should appear on the Stage and increase each time the player hits an enemy with a laser blast. The only thing I don't like is the position of the *Score* and *Lives* counters on the Stage. Fortunately, you can drag a variable to any place you want. I prefer my game variables along the top of the screen.

1 **On the Stage, click and drag the *Lives* display to the top-right side.**

2 **Click and drag the *Score* display to the top-left side.**

Time to invite your friends to try out your game. If it's too easy, you can speed up the aliens or slow the spaceship. Too hard? Allow players to fire their lasers more quickly!

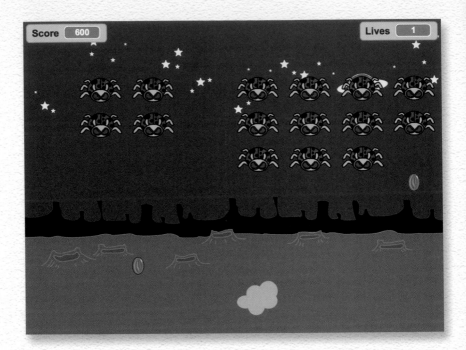

Score 600 Lives 1

You can use the techniques in this project to design just about any shooter game you can imagine. You also could invert the gameplay by making a game in which the player has to catch objects falling from the sky or in which the player has the role of the aliens instead of the spaceship.

So many possibilities when YOU are in control of the game-making! Now close this book and go make a TOTALLY NEW kind of game!!!

ENHANCE YOUR GAME

Here are some ways you might improve your space blaster game.

- » **Animate enemies:** In addition to moving left and right, you could switch between costumes to make the legs move.

- » **Add additional levels:** You could create a new variable named Enemies that tracks the number of enemies left on the screen. When Enemies = 0, you could use a BROADCAST block to create another set of enemies, perhaps changing their appearance or movement.

- » **Gradually change enemy speed:** Like the original arcade game, you could increase the enemy's speed as the number of enemies onscreen decreases.

- » **Add more sound effects:** You could have a marching effect that plays faster as the enemies speed up. Having an end-of-game sound (try Spiral) could be fun, too.

- » **Time delay fuse:** You could have the bombs land on the ground and wait a second or two before exploding.

- » **Add power-ups:** Occasionally, you could have a special enemy bomb with a different costume fall; catching this bomb could add a life or give the player a more powerful laser for a short time.

AUTHOR NOTES

SHARE YOUR SCRATCH PROJECTS ONLINE

By default, you are the only person who can see your Scratch projects. To allow other Scratch users to view, remix and add your project to their studio, you must enable sharing. Sharing a project makes it available to all users around the world, so you should delete any personal information or other elements (spare sprites/blocks/sounds) you do not want strangers to see. If your project is not yet complete, click the Draft checkbox before sharing it to inform people it is a work in process.

SHARE PROJECT FROM ONLINE SCRATCH EDITOR

1 Go to **scratch.mit.edu** and log into your account.

2 Click the My Stuff **button near the top right part of the web page.**

3 You can tell which projects you have already shared by reading the information on the far right. If a project has not been shared, you will see the option to *delete* your project. If it has been shared, you will see the *unshare* option.

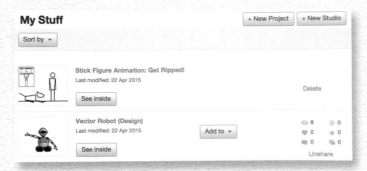

4 **Click the title of the project you wish to share.**

5 **Click the** Share **button.**

6 **Fill out the Instructions and Notes and Credits boxes and choose 1 to 3 tags.**

SHARE PROJECT FROM OFFLINE SCRATCH EDITOR

If you are using the offline Scratch editor, click the File menu and choose *Share to Website*. You will need to log in with your Scratch account, then follow steps 2–6 above.

PUBLISH SCRATCH GAMES ON ANY WEBSITE

While sharing a Scratch project will allow logged in Scratch users to view and remix your projects, you can also display working Scratch projects on your own blog or other website. This is particularly useful for Scratch games which you might want to share with a wider audience.

1 Go to scratch.mit.edu and log into your account.

2 Click the My Stuff button near the top right part of the web page.

3 Click the title of the project you wish to share on another website.

4 If the project has not yet been shared, click the Share button.

5 Click the Embed button.

6 Select and copy the embed html code.

7 Paste the code into your external blog or website.

DEDICATION

For Mom — thank you for all those quarters!

ABOUT THE AUTHOR/DESIGNER

Derek is a founding member of the Instructional Design and Interactive Education Media Association (IDIEM) and is an active member of the Scratch Educator (ScratchEd) community. Most recently, he worked as a graphic designer for the StarLogo Nova project at MIT, as a teaching fellow in Instructional Design at Harvard Extension school, and as a curriculum developer for i2 Camp. He is also an ambassador for Europe Code Week (codeweek.eu) and Africa Code Week (africacodeweek.org).

AUTHOR'S ACKNOWLEDGMENTS

Thank you to the editorial staff at Wiley, especially Amy Fandrei and my Wiley hero Brian Walls.

Without the pioneering work of the Lifelong Kindergarten Group at the MIT Media Lab, I would just be scratching my head (and wishing for something like Scratch to fill my head with tinkering ideas). Thank you Mitchel and Natalie and dozens of people who have worked with them on developing Scratch and sustaining the online community.

I am grateful to Daniel Wendel, Wendy Huang and Josh Sheldon for showing me the true power of blocks-based programming and Eric Klopfer for hiring me into the StarLogo family.

I am continually inspired by educational technology colleagues in Massachusetts, New York, and beyond, especially Cynthia Solomon, Margaret Minsky, Karen Brennan, Sharon Thompson, Keledy Kenkel, Stephen Lewis, Andrea Meyer, Horst Jens, Martin Wollenberger, Claude Terosier, Joek van Montfort and Stephen Howell.

The vibrant folks in IDIEM (Instructional Design and Interactive Education Media Association) gave me to confidence to take on this project, especially my good friends Chad Kirchner, Julie Mullen, Diana Ouellette, Ben Mojica, Karen Motley, Jason Alvarez, Jean Devine and Steve Gordon.

I am also indebted to the fabulous ED103 and ED113 courses at Harvard Extension School, under the masterful direction of Stacie Cassat Green and Denise Snyder.

There would have been far fewer tips and tricks throughout the book were it not for the invaluable Scratch Wiki (www.wiki.scratch.mit.edu) and Scratch Discussion Forums (www.scratch.mit.edu/discuss).

Then there are the Onoratos . . . the Breens . . . the Dowdens . . . the Nangeronis and the Tupelo-Schnecks for ALWAYS being there!

PUBLISHER'S ACKNOWLEDGMENTS

Acquisitions Editor: Amy Fandrei

Project Editor: Brian H. Walls

Scratch Logo: Courtesy of Mitchel Resnick, Lifelong Kindergarten Group, MIT Media Lab

Chapter figures, illustrations, and Scratch projects: Copyright © 2016 Derek Breen

Scratch is developed by the Lifelong Kindergarten Group at the MIT Media Lab. See http://scratch.mit.edu.